Seasons

of

Our Lives

by Glenda Allen Chatham

6. 3. 14

Jeanne,
may God bless you
in each season of
your life.
Glenda

Ps. 138

Library of Congress Control Number: 2003095417
ISBN: 978-0-9744085-0-7

Scripture quotations are from the King James Version KJV
and the New International Version NIV of the HOLY BIBLE.
The NIV is quoted within the amount granted without express
written permission.

Scripture quotations marked (NIV) are taken from the
HOLY BIBLE, NEW INTERNATIONAL VERSION®.
NIV®. Copyright©1973, 1978, 1984, by International Bible
Society. Used by permission of Zondervan. All rights reserved.

The following poems by Glenda Allen Chatham are found in
her previous book, *Timepieces*: "The Dogwood," "Changes,"
"The Other Side of The Clouds," "The Mighty Ocean," "In
Different Shoes," and "Life Is A Gift."

Printed in the United States by
Morris Publishing
3212 East Highway 30
Kearney, NE 68847
1-800-650-7888

Dedication

This book is dedicated to my Savior and Lord Jesus Christ,
Who died for me and prepared the way for eternal life with Him after I have been through the Seasons of My Life here on earth.

Love,
Glenda

Special thanks...
To my husband Fred who encourages me and accepts me for who I am, for my dad who taught me to look up scriptures for myself, and my mother who shows her love for the Lord.

Thanks to Marge Swaim for giving her time to proof read my book and to Neal Weaver for special advice.

TABLE OF CONTENTS

"To everything there is a season, and a time to every purpose under the heaven."
Ecclesiastes 3:1 KJV

Seasons of Our Lives

As a young person I could not wait until I grew up so I could be who I was supposed to be. When in elementary school I couldn't wait until I started to high school. Then I couldn't wait until I started to college. I counted the months until I was to marry the man I met there. After raising my family and teaching school for twenty-seven years I retired. One day I said, "I can't wait until I turn sixty-two so I can draw my Social Security. My nine year old granddaughter, Miriam said, "Grandmama, Don't grow up too fast." WHOA! Let me back up. At what age will I be when I fulfill God's purpose for my life?

During a family Christmas devotion time I asked everyone what they would want someone to say about them behind their back. When it became seven-year old Anna's time to tell she said she would want other's to say that she loved Jesus. What a testimony from someone so young. Is she already being what God wants her to be? Have I been doing it all along? Did I mess up along the way? Is it too late? Does God have different plans for us during the **Seasons of Our Lives?**

Seasons Of Our Lives

God has a calling for us
In all the seasons of our lives.
We need to watch and listen.
With His guidance we will arrive.

Forgetting what lies behind us
And straining forward to what lies ahead,
We can reap the prizes of our calls
If we have truly been God led.

We have many callings
In the pages of our times.
These don't always happen
At periods we consider our prime.

Jesus loves us as little children
And can use the smallest heart.
With God in control of planning
There is no unimportant part.

No matter where we are
Or what our past has been,
God can clean us up
And let us begin again.

"But this one thing I do, forgetting those things which are behind, and reaching forth unto those things which are before, I press toward the mark for the prize of the high calling of God in Christ Jesus." Phil.3: 13-14 KJV

The Dogwood

After many years of enjoying the beauty of a large Dogwood tree, disease and weather took its toll. As much as we disliked the idea we had to cut it down. I was so thrilled to see new branches sprouting out of the trunk a couple of years later. Now even more time has passed and though it is not as big as it once was it again is producing beautiful blossoms. Isn't it wonderful that the most High God is the God of second chances? Just as we often are cut down God can pick us up and use us again for His glory if He so chooses. We too can produce new blossoms as did **The Dogwood.**

The Dogwood

There once was a beautiful Dogwood tree
In the backyard.
It was a lovely sight to view
Until weather battered and scarred.

It had lifted its adorned branches
Up to the sky;
As one of God's pieces of work,
It tried to exemplify.

As time went by,
Its limbs did slump.
The tree was cut down
And became a stump.

Two years have past
And now it's spring.
Out of that old stump
Comes a wonderful thing.

New life is growing.
Blossomed branches uplift.
. God again is giving
Us a glorious gift.

"The command to leave the stump of the tree with its roots means that your kingdom will be restored to you when you acknowledge that Heaven rules." Dan. 4:26 NIV

Pruning! Does It Hurt?

As a student and as a teacher I have taken and given tests. Test time is not the most enjoyable time in life, but it is a good way of seeing how well equipped we are in certain areas. If we were never asked to use the knowledge we have acquired or draw from our experiences, of what use were they? **Pruning! Does It Hurt?**

Pruning! Does It Hurt?

Lord, Sometimes I hurt
And have lots of pain.
I want to trust You
And not complain.

Do You hear my cries
And know that I need pruning?
Are You there
To give me a fine-tuning?

Often I feel that
Life is out of control.
I hurt deep within.
Both heart and soul.

I know the pain
Suffered during childbirth.
I know the joys
Of being given a rebirth.

You know the pain
Caused by the prodigal son.
Does pruning take place
When we are hurt by loved ones?

Is it a reminder
Of what I put You through?
Are You telling me that
Fellowship with You is long overdue?

To often I want to be in charge
And have control.
I want my way
And set my own goal.

When the mountain
Is too steep to climb,
Are You pruning me so I will
Take one day at a time?

Lord, When I don't understand
And send out a fleece,
Are You saying listen
And I'll give you peace?

Lord, When You're Pruning.
Not trying to destroy,
Help me to understand that
Your ways bring blossoms of joy.

"I am the true vine, and my Father is the gardener. He cuts off every branch that bears no fruit, while every branch that does bear fruit he prunes so that it will be even more fruitful. You are already clean because of the word I have spoken to you. Remain in me, and I will remain in you. No branch can bear fruit by itself; it must remain in the vine. Neither can you bear fruit unless you remain in me. I am the vine; you are the branches.

If a man remains in me and I in him, he will bear much fruit; apart from me, he is like a branch that is thrown away and withers; such branches are picked up, thrown into the fire and burned. If you remain in me and my words in you, ask whatever you wish, and it will be given you. This is to my Father's glory, that you bear much fruit, showing yourselves to be my disciples."
John 15:1-8 NIV

Morning Walk With The Lord

Sometimes life seems like a game of Dodge Ball with everything coming at us at once. Satan strikes us where we are the most vulnerable. As Matthew 10:21 tells us brothers will betray one another. Even parents and children will hurt one another. Brothers and sisters in Christ, who should set an example of Christian love, fight while a lost world looks on. I was pondering on some of these things during a stay on the coast of Florida. It was September 11, 2001. While watching the news I suddenly viewed two planes go into the Twin Towers in New York. Now a year and a half later our nation is at war in Iraq.

We need to wake up. God desires fellowship with each of us. We need a **Morning Walk With The Lord.**

Morning Walk With The Lord

This morning I walked alone the shore
With many waves of doubt.
I cried aloud unto the Lord
And ask what life was all about.

Satan had attacked my family, my church,
And now my own homeland.
Was God telling me to watch for Him,
That the rapture was close at hand?

As I searched for my seashells,
I desired more than just the ordinary.
I looked more deeply into the sand.
Was I looking as close as necessary?

I also wanted more than an ordinary
Walk with my Jesus Lord and Savior.
I wanted a walk that pleased Him.
I wanted one without doubts and waiver.

The disciples often doubted
And didn't understand what Jesus told,
But after the Day of Pentecost
The Holy Spirit made them bold.

I asked the Lord for that boldness
In all my future walks.
I asked Him to take and use me as He willed.
And with me have constant talks.

``And they heard the voice of the Lord God walking in the garden in the cool of the day:''
Gen. 3:8a KJV

``And I will walk among you, and will be your God, and ye shall be my people.'' Ps. 138:7 KJV

``Though I walk in the midst of trouble, Thou wilt revive me: thou shalt stretch forth thine hand against the wrath of mine enemies, and thy right hand shall save me.''
Lev. 26:12 KJV

11

An On Time God

I am not the most patient person in the world, but I am trying to change. God does not have to prove anything to me. His ways are not the same as mine; but as I look back over the years, He has never failed me. He has never given me anything that was harmful or kept anything from me that I needed. He has always been **An On Time God.**

An On Time God

Sometimes I grow impatient
When waiting on the Lord.
I forget He never fails me.
If I trust, there's great reward.

He's an on time God.
Never has He been late.
From me He wants my fellowship.
With me He wants to communicate.

When I want to rush things
And have them 'yesterday',
God reminds me of His wish
For me to trust and obey.

He's an on time God.
He is never late.
Some answers are yes and no.
Others are simply wait.

"Rest in the Lord, and wait patiently for Him." Ps.37: 7a
KJV

13

"Wait on the Lord: be of good courage, and he shall strengthen thine heart: wait, I say, on the Lord." Ps. 27:14KJV

"Let integrity and uprightness preserve me, for I wait on thee." Ps. 25:21 KJV

"Lead me in thy truth, and teach me: for thou art the God of my salvation; on thee do I wait all the day." Ps. 25:5 KJV

The Battle

It is hard to share some of our personal experiences we have with God and we don't always need to share those most intimate times, but one evening I felt a strong presence of both God and Satan. I felt I was in the mist of a violent conflict. Satan appeared very strong, but I saw who won **The Battle**. I have drawn from that experience many times. I have found the more we stay in God's word the more experiences we have to draw from.

The Battle

Sometimes we struggle with battles within.
There is the temptation to do wrong, a force called
sin.
Satan loves to go on his rampages
As he has done through out the ages.

God is different. He shows great love.
The greatest was when He sent His Son from
above.
Satan is strong and has great powers.
His control is mighty and always devours.

He causes lives to be in an upheaval.
Whatever his appearance, it is always evil.
But, no matter how much Satan tries,
There's soon to be a great war cry.

God Almighty is in control.
Life is not without reason. God has a goal.
Satan too has made his plans.
In the Garden of Eden is when they began.

God's Son Jesus has paid the cost.
The battle with sin is already lost.
For each person who comes back as the prodigal son,
Hasn't a worry. His battle is won.

God's Son Jesus
Will come again without fail.
The battle will be over.
God will prevail.

"These shall make war with the Lamb, and the Lamb shall overcome them: for He is Lord of lords, and King of kings: and they that are with Him are called, and chosen, and faithful."   Rev. 17:14 KJV

Two Roads

When traveling in Montana my husband and I chose the scenic route from Great Falls to Yellowstone, Wyoming. Nature was unspoiled. There wasn't the noise and traffic one would find on the Express Way. It wasn't always convenient to be so isolated. The luxury of restrooms, fast food restaurants, and stations for fuel were long and far between. Oh but, the beauty made it worth it all. Because of God's grace I have chosen the better of **Two Roads.**

Two Roads

There is a picture I would like to draw.
It is of two roads. One is narrow and the other is
broad.
The broad has laughter and seems inviting
With many faces, happy and exciting.

But, it is the narrow on which I set my sights.
With Jesus before me, He gives it light.
The narrow is steep and often forlorn,
One less traveled, with rocks and thorns.

With Jesus as the light for each step ahead,
His hand will guide me. There is nothing to dread.
Oh the beauty at the end of that road
Is more than anyone in this life will ever behold.

"Enter ye in at the strait gate: for wide is the gate, and broad is the way, that leadeth to destruction, and many there be that go in thereat: Because strait is the gate, and narrow is the way, which leadeth unto life, and few there be that find it." Matt. 7:13-14 KJV

Opportunities To Trust

Oh how I must hurt God by not trusting in Him. When my children were growing up in a house, which had more than one level one of my daughters would say, Mama, "Will you watch me as I go upstairs?" How could she have been so afraid going somewhere in her own home? Her dad and I were there. The doors were locked. The lights were on. We wouldn't let anyone hurt her. She was very loved. She had many **Opportunities to Trust.**

Opportunities To Trust

Thank You Lord
For opportunities to trust in You,
As did Noah
When commanded to gather the animals two by two.

When troubles come
Help us to give You thanks,
When we have no answers
And our minds are blank.

Without You as Lord
Life would be like leaning on the web of a spider.
With You as Lord
We can know You as the great provider.

As we go through life
And times seem unclear,
Remind us that
We are to trust and not to fear.

Your children are not
As grass without water.
Each one of us is
A special son or daughter.

As part of Your family
We are not without hope.
You are always there
To help us cope.

Your Word says when afraid
We are to trust in Thee.
You never sleep.
We have Your guarantee.

So help us Lord
When we have our scares
To know You are with us.
We can communicate in prayer.

When we feel desperate
In a world situation,
Help us remember
Our promised destination.

Whether above the clouds
Or on a stormy sea
We know we can
Always count on Thee.

We need to come
To the end of ourselves
Before we can truly rely
On You Lord to be Yourself.

Thank You Lord
For opportunities to trust in You.
Thank You for always
Seeing us through.

"Mine enemies would daily swallow me up: for they be many that fight against me, O thou most High. What time I am afraid, I will trust in thee. In God I will praise his word, in God I have put my trust; I will not fear what flesh can do unto me." Ps. 56:2-4 KJV

Life's Treasures

I have heard the statement that the best things in life are free. People have made life complicated. The joy has gone out of things. My grandmother used to put a big button on a string. I would be entertained for hours making that button spin and hum. Years ago I decided to start giving my third graders big wooden buttons (made by my husband) on a strong piece of cord as Christmas gifts. After teaching them how to get them spinning and humming without getting caught in someone's hair sitting nearby I had a hard time making them store them away. I forbid them to bring them back into the classroom. Even though given expensive toys at Christmas, their parents shared with me how they continued to play with the buttons. What has happened to us? Where are our priorities? God paid the biggest price of all for a gift for us. We only have to receive it. SALVATION. It's free. It is the greatest of **Life's Treasures.**

Life's Treasures

We should be thankful for
All life's treasures.
What really counts
Is hard to measure.

We need to feel close and
Have the touch of a hand.
We need to believe in something
And take a stand.

Talking to God
Is our greatest gift,
A privilege given
That will always uplift.

It is good to take time
To be with a friend,
To be able to share differences
And not offend.

What's one man's junk
Is another man's treasure.
Even an old book
Can bring much pleasure.

Life itself is a treasure
We don't need to waste.
We need to go slow
And not at fast pace.

We shouldn't worry.
We've only one life to live.
We should never hold grudges.
We should always forgive.

Enjoying the sunshine
And a walk in the rain
Can make life easier
And take away strain.

Seeing the dusk of day
And a beautiful sunrise
Can be more important
Than winning a first prize.

It's fun to be in a rocker
Or an old porch swing
And spot a flower
Bringing the first sign of spring.

Seeing morning glories on a fence
And smelling sweet honeysuckle
Should make our hearts sing
And let out a chuckle.

Climbing a mountain
And seeing a waterfall
Makes the day a success
And worth it all.

"For God so loved the world, that he gave his only begotten Son, that whosoever believeth in him should not perish, but have everlasting life."   John 3:16KJV

A Little Bit of Yesterday

I have a picture hanging on my kitchen wall. The family in the picture is at a table. The mother and children are sitting while the dad is standing. All have bowed heads. Is there a need for a table in today's time? How often do parents and their children eat together around the table in their home? During the evening meal families used to discuss events that had happened during the day. Television commercials now laugh off the eating together at the breakfast table as Mom throws breakfast bars to her teenager and husband as they pass through to say goodbye for the day. There also used to be a gathering for Bible reading before bedtime each evening.

Children grow up fast parents. Do you know your children? Do they know you? What are your priorities? Do we need **A Little Bit of Yesterday**?

A little Bit Of Yesterday

Do we need a little bit of yesterday?
What draws us back?
What's wrong with today?
Why are we ready to attack?

Was yesterday really that good,
All happy and warm?
Did the day have fewer problems?
Were there fewer storms?

Was life better when the family
Ate together at the dinner table?
Was there something there
That made them more stable?

Was there less violence
When parents took time?
When the Bible was read
Did we see less crime?

Was there more respect for life
And love for our brother?
Did we look after number one
Or did we look after each other?

Where are we going?
Why do we fuss?
What is life about?
What frightens us?

Could we break the vicious cycle
And life's trying demands
By turning back to God
And placing our lives in His hands?

``And thou shalt return and obey the voice of the Lord, and do all his commandments which I command thee this day.'' Deut. 30: 8 KJV

Do What I Can

I have always enjoyed the ocean. I used to love the feel of waves lifting me up and dropping me on the other side. Occasionally a wave would break, crashing down on me, but it was worth the chance of the ride. Oh how I loved that experience, but now I find myself frightened. What if I can't get back up after being knocked down? What if I drown? What if the tide pulls me out to far to get back? I just need to **Do What I Can.**

Do What I Can

Now that I am getting to
Be a little older in age,
I find there are things
In which I cannot engage.

Maybe I need to accept age more gracefully
And do what I can.
Maybe there is something different
And I need another plan.

I may not be able to climb a mountain,
But I can climb a hill.
Smelling the flowers along the way
Can bring a pleasant thrill.

I may have stopped working
And be considered retired,
But I can always be used
In my own church choir.

My muscles may stiffen
And have more aches,
But I can always take
My lounge chair and sit by the lake.

I don't have to run races
And lay in the sun.
I can even let some of
My work go undone.

I don't have to be scared and
Feel that I am impaired.
God enjoys me coming
To Him in prayer.

I will always need goals
And some kind of plan.
I just need to remember
It is okay to do what I can.

"And we know that all things work together for good to them that love God, to them who are called according to his purpose." Rom.8: 28 KJV

I Can Choose

There is a saying I have heard since childhood: "You shouldn't cry over spilled milk."

A couple of days after I wrote the poem "**I Can Choose**", I backed my car out of my new garage. Until a week before it had been a carport so I just happened to forget to put the door up. The man who had installed the door thought it much funnier than I did. I gave him a copy of my poem along with his payment. Talk about being tested!

I Can Choose

I can choose whether to worry and be depressed,
Or I can choose to look to God and know that I
am blessed.
I can choose to be happy and content
By remembering what my Savior underwent.

I can choose the words I say.
I can always go to God and pray.
I can choose a better life to live.
I need to be willing to forgive.

I don't have to struggle and fight.
If I listen, God will give insight.
If things happen to make me sad,
God can remind me that life's not bad.

I can choose. I have a choice.
With God's help I can rejoice.

"Speaking to yourselves in psalms and hymns and spiritual songs, singing and making melody in your heart to the Lord; Giving thanks always for all things unto God and the Father in the name of our Lord Jesus Christ;" Eph. 5:19-20 KJV

I Trust My Pilot. He Charts My Path

I love to fly. You know, ``Just sit back and leave the driving to us.'' I have never had any bad experiences with flying. Even when going through some turbulence one trip I didn't worry because I saw a pilot in uniform taking my flight as a passenger. The turbulence didn't seem to faze him at all as I watched him. I thought, ``Why should I be afraid if He's not.''

One of my favorite passages of scripture is in Psalms 139. God knew me before I was ever formed, even when I was just a thought in His mind. I am never out of His sight. He even knows the number of hairs on my head and that changes daily on my husband's head. Having God as my guide, I need to remember to **Trust My Pilot. He Charts My Path.**

I Trust My Pilot. He Charts My Path.

I love to travel. I love to fly.
God's handiwork is manifested in the sky.
I trust my Pilot. My path He doth chart.
He knows all about me. He even knows my heart.

My Pilot knows my destination.
I am special. I am His creation.
When the journey is rough and there are turbulences,
My Pilot knows everything about my circumstances.

My Pilot knows my every thought.
He doesn't want me to be distraught.
He was there when I was shaped and formed.
He is certainly there when there are storms.

My Pilot knows my most inward parts.
He has been there with me from the start.
When He is up in the cockpit,
He wants me to relax and solely submit.

Whether I am in the heavens or in the deepest seas,
My Pilot wants me to be worry free.
He knows when I sit and when I stand.
He is right there with me to hold my hand.

He charts my path. He knows the way.
He loves my company. He wants me to pray.
God is my Pilot. He is in command.
He has control. He understands.

All I have to do is on Him rely.
In all ways He will supply.

"O Lord, thou hast searched me, and known me. Thou knowest my downsitting and mine uprising, thou compassest my path and my lying down, and art acquainted with all my ways.
If I ascend up into heaven, thou art there: if I make my bed in hell, behold thou art there. If I take the wings of the morning, and dwell in the uttermost parts of the sea; even there shall thy hand lead me, and thy right hand shall hold me." Ps. 139:1-3, 8-10 KJV

My Computer

I have a problem of being obsessive. I can't get things off my mind. It can be about something good as well as bad, but it still takes up too much of my time.

God made computers way before man thought he invented them. I don't know much about man made computers, but I do know they have an allotted amount of space on the Hard Drive and can crash if overloaded. I learned this when scanning too many pictures into my computer.

I use to tell my students that just as we would not feed our bodies poison, neither should we read nor watch things on television that are trash because once in our minds it is hard to erase. I have found this true with my problem of obsession. If I see or read something that is bad it is hard to delete. I need to be careful what I allow to enter **My Computer**.

My Computer

When God made my body
He gave me a brain.
He created it
Without blemish or stain.

I shouldn't feed it
Trash and things that are bad.
This makes God
Very sad.

The Bible says a man is as
He thinketh in his heart.
I don't want my God and I
To ever be apart.

So Lord, I pray that
You will help keep my mind clean.
Don't let things of this world
For You and I come between.

"Create in me a clean heart, O God; and renew a right spirit within me." Ps.51: 10 KJV
"For as he thinketh in his heart, so is he." Prov.23: 7 KJV

Problems

I memorized scripture as a child and one verse that comes to my mind when times are frightening is "What time I am afraid I will trust in Thee." No problem I have had has ever come to stay. I cannot look back and see anytime God has failed to see me through my **Problems.**

Problems

Father, give me the faith to trust You more
As I place my problems into Your hands.
Protect and guide me down the right path.
Help me to let go and let You be in command.

If that path seems rocky and forlorn
And my heart feels that it is breaking,
Remind me that You are all knowing
And someday there will be a great awakening.

Help me use my time wisely
And continually be in prayer with You.
Give me strength and patience,
Knowing You will always see me through.

"Though now for a little while you may have had to suffer grief in all kinds of trials. These have come so that your faith-of greater worth than gold, which perishes even though refined by fire-may be proved genuine and may result in praise, glory and honor when Jesus Christ is revealed." 1 Peter 1:4-6b NIV

Keep Going! Don't Quit!

The formation of a pearl begins when a substance that is foreign to the oyster gets between its mantle and shell. The mantle covers the irritant with the same substance that is in the shell. Eventually a pearl is formed from this reaction. If we continue to work with the irritations we have in life with the help of our Lord, He can make pearls through our reactions. If we don't give up and continue to grow in the Lord something beautiful can happen in our lives also. We need remember to **Keep Going! Don't Quit!**

Keep Going! Don't Quit!

Keep going. Don't quit.
Life's hard, but don't just sit.
Remember how the oyster makes a pearl.
Keep working with the irritations in this world.
You could be receiving an unexpected gift,
One to share with others: Their spirits to uplift.
When you struggle and your heart breaks,
Remember past blessings and take a break.
Feel the wind blow. Smell the flowers.
Remember God and all His powers.
Don't quit. Just keep going.
You may find that you are growing.

"Watch ye, stand fast in the faith, quit you like men, be strong." 1 Cor.16: 13 KJV

God Is In Control

Control!   Control can be such an ugly thing when wrongly used.   People often want to control the lives of others.   They think they know best when maybe they don't know all the facts.   Even if all facts are known, who is to be in control of another person?   God certainly expects parents to take care of their children when young and children their parents when old, but at what age is an individual responsible for himself?

Our world system is very out of control with so many wanting that control.   Our countries are at war with one another.   We have leaders whose people under their dictatorship are being tortured and killed. Our own nation is now threatened in a way it has never known before. It is time we all turn to the one who is in control and ask for His leadership and guidance with our families and our country.

God Is In Control! He is omnipotent! He reigneth!

God Is In Control

Do you hurt?
Are things not as you think they should be?
Have you spoken to God?
Have you been down on your knees?

The devil is at work,
But don't despair.
If you are born again,
God has a great "child care".

No matter what
You feel is going wrong,
If you are His child
You are not alone.

Whatever the problem,
However deep the hole,
God knows all.
God is in control.

"And I heard as it were the voice of a great multitude, and as the voice of many waters, and as the voice of mighty thundering, saying, Alleluia: for the God omnipotent reigneth." Rev. 19:6 KJV

Take Time

I really enjoyed a science class I took a few years back. The teacher had us go out each morning and find a private spot to either write or draw for twenty minutes. He never took up our writings or works of art, but oh, what a pleasant way to begin the class. I could hardly wait to return to that class each day, knowing how it would begin. The teacher made us ``take time''. You could just feel the stressors of life leave as you found some wild flowers to draw as you sat on a stump or an idea for writing as you sat by a brook watching the water.

My husband and I went camping about three years ago with my parents, my brothers and their wives. I wrote the poem Take Time while I sat by a stream watching the water rush over the rocks and butterflies flitting about. One of my sisters in laws died a sudden death a year ago. I am glad I went camping with her. I'm glad we took a walk. I am glad I remembered to **Take Time.**

Take Time

Take time to hear the gurgle
Of a cool mountain stream.
Take time to sort out priorities
And see what God meant for life to mean.

Take time to watch a
Campfire burn.
See the rocks,
Trees, and ferns.

Take time to see
God's little critters.
Forget those things
That make life bitter.

Take time to look at
The moss on trees and rocks.
Leave behind all
Troubles and clocks.

Find a mountain and
Take a climb.
Leave behind that
Thing called time.

Take time to watch the trees.
See the sun coming through.
Look at the scattered patches
In the sky so blue.

Take time to see
A perched butterfly.
Take time to live
Before you die.

"And He said unto them. Come ye yourselves apart into a desert place, and rest awhile." Mark 6:31 KJV

Changes

After taking the same route year after year to my job I had to change because of construction on the road. I found myself having to take side roads and going an extra mile. What seem to be an inconvenience became pleasant. I saw flowers and trees that were not along the main road. I enjoyed the change. Not all **Changes** are bad.

Changes

Sometime obstacles
May block our passage;
But if we seek another way,
It could be to our advantage.

We may have to change
And reroute for awhile.
It may be hard to understand
Having to take the extra mile.

There could be beauty in new routes,
Though they may take longer.
God could use them
To make us grow stronger.

New experiences could make
Life more interesting.
What first seems like a burden,
Could become a blessing.

So when routes in our lives
Make a sudden change,
Remember our vision is limited,
But God's view is long range.

"O Lord, I know that the way of man is not in himself: it is not in man that walketh to direct his steps." Jer. 10:23 KJV

God Wants Our Attention

My husband is a light sleeper, but one night when I was having a spell of asthma he did not wake up. It seemed the louder I wheezed the sounder he slept. He had always been there for me before. I felt hurt. I got up and went into the den. There I cried out to the Lord. He heard my cry. He said, "I am here." I rested in His arms. **God Wants Our Attention.**

God Wants Our Attention

God wants our attention.
He has His ways.
He will remove all others
And make us pray.

He will keep a close mate
From hearing our cries.
Friends will be to busy
Until God gets a reply.

God is not punishing us
Or Being unkind,
But He is a jealous God
And wants to be our lifeline.

God does often use hands
Of Christian sisters and brothers,
But reminds us at times that
He is our one and only.
There is none other.

``Do we provoke the Lord to jealousy?'' 1 Cor. 10:22a KJV
``I am jealous for you with a godly jealousy.'' 2 Cor. 11:2a
NIV

Watering Our Roots

I know very little about plants, but I do know they have to be given water or they will die. I used to do a science activity with my students. Everyone had to put the tree cookie they had drawn on the ground and place one foot on it. That foot was not to move. They could reach out with their hands for colored Popsicle sticks that I threw at them. The Popsicle sticks were blue representing water, green representing nutrients, and yellow representing sunshine. Jesus refers to Himself as living water in John 4:10 and again as the water of life in Revelations 21:6. Psalms 27:1 says the Lord is our light and our salvation. John 6:35 tells us that Jesus is also the bread of life. Just as the students needed all three colors of sticks to survive in the science activity or they were out, we need the water, bread, and light Jesus offers. If we are to survive in any relationship we need to nurture it with the right ingredients. We need to keep **Watering Our Roots.**

Watering Our Roots

My husband and I gathered together
With college friends, forty years from our past.
Now we still try to see one another,
Nurturing relationships that continue to last.
It's like cultivating the soil
And watering the roots.
The gift of a friend
Is better than delicious fruits.

Studying God's word and
Walking daily with the Lord
Will make one reap
A greater reward.
Nurturing 'that' relationship
And watering those roots
Will produce abundant growth
For which there is no substitute.

"Study to shew thyself approved unto God, a workman that needeth not to be ashamed, rightly dividing the word of truth." 2 Tim. 2:15 KJV

What Do People See When They Look At Me?

My husband and I were babysitting three of our granddaughters last night. Music was on and twenty-month-old Naomi was dancing around with her sisters. She was trying to do what they did. I started rolling my hands and then putting them up in the air. Naomi quickly added this to her dance routine. I thought of some of the things I do wrong. I have several bad habits that I need to work on. I wouldn't want those habits imitated by my grandchildren. I want to set a good example.

What Do People See When They Look At Me?

56

What Do People See When They Look At Me?

What do people see
When they look at me?
Do they see someone who conforms
In the mist of life's storms?

In public, how am I viewed?
When among strangers, am I rude?
Am I ever one to judge?
When wronged, do I hold a grudge?

Do I often like to criticize?
Am I slow to apologize?
Are there some people I avoid
And with others act overjoyed?

Am I controlling and aggressive?
Do things get out of hand and I become excessive?
When I want my way and have to have the lead
Am I really just showing greed?

What do people see in me?
Is it what Jesus would have me be?
With others am I quick to embrace?
Does my face show I've experienced God's loving
grace?

Do I ever give others a compliment?
When around me, do they feel content?
What kind of fruit do I bear?
Do people see me as one who cares?
What do people see when they look at me?

"Wherefore by their fruits ye shall know them."
Matt. 7:20 KJV

Nudges From Above

Sometimes I want things to have a title. When I was a young teenager I felt God was possibly calling me to be a missionary in the jungle. I was told I didn't have to wait until I finished school and went to college. I was told that I could be a missionary right then. I never went to the jungle, but I did teach school and it often felt like I was in the jungle. Even since I have retired I have asked God if He has a job for me to do. I wonder if I am listening or if I am still looking for a title. Could He be telling me something when everyday needs arrive with **Nudges From Above**?

Nudges From Above

Lord, I didn't go to a foreign field
And become a missionary.
I've lived many years, but
Have never done anything extraordinary.

I want to be productive,
But sometimes don't know what to do.
When I think to visit a shut-in,
Is that a little nudge from You?

I feel so self-centered
And often full of greed.
I want to be more useful
And do someone a good deed.

When I know of someone sick
And fix a meal or just a stew,
Dear Lord, am I doing that because I had a nudge
from You?

If someone is in the hospital
and I take them a flower,
Does it help them if I sit there quietly
And give them just an hour?

Telling others who is responsible
When sharing a panoramic view,
Is that the Holy Spirit
Sending me another nudge from You?

Lord, I know You love me
And always had me in Your mind.
Help me feel the nudges
That You have to me assigned.

"Just as each of us has one body with many members, and these members do not have the same function, so in Christ we who are many form one body, and each member belongs to all the others. We have different gifts, according to the grace given us." Rom.12: 4-6b NIV

Life's Journey

God has blessed me with the chance to travel during the past few years. I have seen the alpines in Germany and taken walks in the Black Forrest. I have seen snow capped glaciers in Montana and stood on cliffs overlooking the ocean in California. I have watched Old Faithful go off in Wyoming and sat beside a gurgling mountain stream in my own state of Georgia. I have watched boats come into dock in small fishing villages in Maine and taken the loop at Acadia Park. I have stood in awe looking at God's handiwork. I can't imagine what heaven will look like, but I do believe the best is yet to come. I am thankful for my **Life's Journey**.

Life's Journey

Lord, I love to travel
And see what Your hands have made.
It is awesome to see areas
That man has not been allowed to invade.

I have seen rocks beaten
By the strong ocean waves.
I have seen beautiful formations
Hanging from the ceilings of caves.

Lord, You've carved out valleys
And capped glaciers with snow.
You've allowed me to see these
And also crystal clear coves.

I have seen Yellowstone's mysterious geysers
And sparkling water falls.
God, You have let me
See them all.

Some Sequoia trees are many
Thousands of years old.
I have viewed them as
They stand so tall and bold.

Lord, I am thankful
For the beauty on this earth,
But nothing can compare
With the gift of rebirth.

With this gift comes
The promise of being with You.
I can't even grasp
What I will then be able to view.

Thank You, God for the opportunities
You have given me down here,
But help me to remember during the storms of life
That You are also very near.

As I journey through life
I want to see and learn something new everyday.
Most important, I want to remember that
In God's presence is the most awesome place to stay.

``And one cried unto another, and said, Holy, holy, holy, is the Lord of hosts: the whole earth is fill of his glory." Isa.6: 3 KJV
``Thus saith the Lord, The heaven is my throne, and the earth is my footstool." Isa. 66:1a KJV

God's Light

A few years ago my granddaughters, Ashley, age six, and Alisha, age 3, were spending the night with their granddaddy and me. They said they were afraid to sleep upstairs. I gave them a flashlight and told them it would burn out if they used it too much, but that God's light would never burn out. The next morning little Alisha came down the stairs with a burned out flashlight. She said, "God's light didn't burn out." I was so proud she remembered. She also said she was glad God made Ashley or she would have been "scareder." Ashley and Alisha's mother is named Faith. I wish I had more "faith" and trust in God and remembered more often that **God's Light** really doesn't ever go out.

God's Light

Light has been important
Since the beginning of time.
To be without it
Has associated darkness with crime.

There is one gift of light
That no one can take away.
It is the gift God gave through His Son Jesus,
When we accept and obey.

The light God gave
Will never cease to glow.
It came in the form of a baby
Two thousand years ago.

"And God said, "Let there be light," and there was light.
God saw that the light was good, and he separated the light
from the darkness." Gen. 1:3-4 NIV

"Though I sit in darkness, the Lord will be my light."
Micah 7:8b NIV

"I have come into the world as a light, so that no one who
believes in me should stay in darkness." John 12:46 NIV

The Other Side Of The Clouds

My first time to fly was July 13, 1990, my 50th birthday. I was on my way to Gothenburg, Sweden. The beauty of the clouds was unlike anything I could imagine. I was in such awe. They looked like huge glaciers of ice and yet did not look cold. I felt as if I were in a fairyland of soft, warm, white waves surrounded by a sea of blue. I was the only passenger with eyes glued to the window for ten hours. How could anyone not believe in the God of Creation? I felt I was just a little closer to heaven on **The Other Side Of The Clouds**.

The Other Side Of The Clouds

The other side of the clouds
Was a beautiful sight.
I flew to another country
During morning and night.

It was my first time to fly
And be on that side.
It was so awesome,
I almost cried.

The clouds looked
Like huge glaciers of ice.
I didn't know God had created
Such a paradise.

The clouds looked like ice,
But they didn't look cold.
They were surrounded by a sea of blue.
It was a sight to behold.

How could anyone not believe
In the God of all creation
After being given
Such an inspiration?

Some day I will again be in the clouds.
I read about it in God's story.
He is coming for me,
And I will be forever with Him in glory.

"Listen, I tell you a mystery: We will not all sleep, but we will all be changed- In a flash, in the twinkling of an eye, at the last trumpet. For the trumpet will sound, the dead will be raised imperishable, and we will be changed." 1 Cor. 15:51-52 NIV

"They will see the Son of Man coming in a cloud with power and great glory." Luke 21:27 NIV

"We who are still alive and are left will be caught up together with them in the clouds to meet the Lord in the air." 1 Thess. 4:17 NIV

"In my Father's house are many rooms; If it were not so, I would have told you. I am going there to prepare a place for you. And if I go and prepare a place for you, I will come back and take you to be with me that you also may be where I am."   John 14:2-3 NIV

The Mighty Ocean

I have always loved the ocean. I love to take early morning walks as the sun is coming up and watch the sea gulls dive down for their breakfast. I used to love to bask in the sun and with eyes closed listen to the breaking waves. I enjoyed riding the waves as they swelled just before they broke. I still like to lay in bed at night listening to that old familiar sound. God who made such a magnificent body of water with its forceful pull of the tides can also speak to it and make a great calm. **The Mighty Ocean**- created by a living God.

The Mighty Ocean

I love the mighty ocean.
I like to jump the waves.
Upon the passing of the years,
I don't feel quite as brave.

I still enjoy walking
And feeling the pulling tide,
And seeing the little sandpipers,
Racing by my side.

Oh, the mighty ocean!
It swells with great strength.
No one can measure
Its magnificent length.

I love to feel the sand,
Warm between my toes.
It also warms my heart
And makes it all aglow.

The seagulls add their music
As they fly overhead.
It doesn't take a morsel of food
To make me feel well fed.

The great mighty ocean
Has always been my friend.
It's another one of God's gifts
That's hard to comprehend.

"O God our Savior, the hope of all the ends of the earth and of the farthest seas...who stilled the roaring of the seas, the roaring of their waves..." Ps. 65:5b, 7a
"Let heaven and earth praise him, the seas and all that move in them." Ps. 69:34a NIV

Be Who You Were Meant To Be

My husband says I beat up on myself. I care too much what others think. God made me special. I only have to answer to Him. If He is pleased then that should be enough. What else really matters? I can only be myself. You can only **Be Who You Were Meant to Be.**

Be Who You Were Meant To Be

When God made you
He had a purpose in mind.
Don't let others put you down.
Remember, you are one of a kind.

Though others may try
to lead you astray,
God made you special.
Look to Him and obey.

Be the person God
Meant for you to be.
Answer only to Him
And be worry-free.

Others may try to belittle
And make you feel small.
Remember your Creator
And stand up tall.

None of God's children
Were born to lose.
He gave each one
Some gift to use.

God made you unique.
On Him, depend.
You will find
Life has great dividends.

"So God created man in his own image, in the image of God created he him; male and female created he them. And God saw everything that he had made and, behold, it was very good." Gen. 1:27, 31 KJV

My Desire For My Children

As an educator I want all of my children and grandchildren to have the education and opportunities to do what they want to do with their lives. I want the best this life has to offer, but without knowledge of Lord as their Savior it would all be in vain. That knowledge is **My Desire For My Children.**

My Desire For My Children

My desire for my children is not for a life that is
carefree.
Neither do they have to go to college and get a
Ph.D.

They don't have to achieve great fortune and fame.
They don't have to go out and make a great name.

I do want my children and grandchildren to do their
best
And give God the credit and know they are blessed.

Power and money are only external.
What I want for my family is something eternal.

My greatest desire is their destination.
It can come about only through God's plan of
salvation.

As a mother and grandmother I often ponder.
I pray, Dear Lord, their lives they won't squander.

My desire for my children and grandchildren is that
they all accept Christ
And seek to serve Him because of what He
sacrificed.

77

"These commandments I give you today are to be upon your hearts. Impress them on your children. Talk about them when you sit at home and when you walk along the road, when you lie down and when you get up. Tie them as symbols on your hands and bind them on your foreheads. Write them on the doorframes of your houses and on your gates." Deut. 6:6-9NIV

Springs In Our Lives

I love new beginnings. God has blessed my husband and me with three daughters and nine granddaughters. It is hard to describe the feelings I had at the time of each one's birth. I love spring when new leaves come on the trees and birds build their nests for their new families' arrival. I used to enjoy the beginning of a new school year with great expectations for my new group of boys and girls. I miss those days of new grandbabies and new students, but even in retirement God gives new adventures and **Springs In Our Lives**.

Springs In Our Lives

A new baby is born,
So tiny and petite.
Relatives and friends say,
Oh how sweet!

Birds fly home
From their winter retreats.
We welcome them back
And inwardly greet.

A new job can be
More than a chore.
It can be a revelation
Of a new open-door.

New beginnings
Are the springs in our lives.
What ever our ages
We need not lose our drive.

Even in retirement
We can make our mark.
There's a world out there
Upon which to embark.

"Being confident of this, that he who began a good work in you will carry it on to completion until the day of Christ Jesus." Phil. 1:6 NIV

Read The Instructions Before All Else Fails

Our world system is in a mess. Everyone seems to have different ideas on how to fix it. Wouldn't it be nice if everyone read the instructions first? Instead many are concerned that to be fair to all we need to take God out of the pledge to our flag, prayer out of the schools, and realize it is not whom we believe in as long as we believe in something?

Where do we find the instructions? Have they been lost? Are they in the Koran? The Book of Mormons? The Bible? Did an idol made by man write them or did someone that is now dead write them? Did a "living God" who still lives write them?

Did the destruction of Sodom and Gomorrah really happen? Could the same happen to us if we do not **Read The Instruction Before All Else Fails?**

Read The Instructions Before All Else Fails

It has been said, when all else fails
Read the instructions.
Why not try a reversal
And skip the destructions.

Read the instructions
Before all else fails.
Go to God's Word.
Look for details.

God wrote His laws in stone.
He expects us to obey.
They were written to protect us
And show us the way.

God never planned
For a life full of stress.
He wants us to read His instructions
And then He will bless.

"The fear of the Lord is the beginning of knowledge: but fools despise wisdom and instruction. My son, hear the instruction of thy father, and forsake not the law of thy mother:" Pro.1: 7-8 KJV

"Take fast hold of instruction: let her not go: keep her; for she is thy life." Pro.4: 13 KJV

"He shall die without instruction; and in his folly he shall go astray." Pro.5: 23 KJV

"Give instruction to a wise man, and he will be yet wiser: teach a just man, and he will increase in learning." Pro.9: 9 KJV

Values

When I first started my teaching career I was able to begin each day with a short Bible Story and the Lord's Prayer. I did not read anything that a denomination different from mine would have objected to. It was a simple story taken from God's Word. I could make the story of Joseph last for days. The students looked forward to the beginning of a new day. Five minutes every morning did not take away time from important studies, but instead prepared students with relaxed minds for learning. If there was a problem to deal with I was backed by the parents. Years later that privilege of reading the Bible Story, having the Lord's Prayer, and a blessing before lunch was taken from my students and me. There started to be more difficult problems to contend with over the years. Often there was not support from the parents. Sometimes there were even threats to me if their children needed correcting. Respect for one another was gone. Later the school system sent out forms asking teachers how they were teaching "**Values**" in the classroom because something needed to be done. I am now retired. I hear that the government may have God taken out of the Pledge to our flag. How sad that our young teachers of today will never know how it used to be.

Values

What are our values?
Are they things of worth?
What has been instilled into us
Since our birth?

Have we been taught
Things that are desirable?
Were they good things,
Easily acquirable?

Who or what has
Determined our life goals?
Will what we've become
Affect our souls?

The lessons we've been taught
And the standards we've held,
Have they made us who we are?
Have they been upheld?

``Those who hope in me will not be disappointed.'' Isa.49:
23c NIV

Consequences

The Lord had Moses send twelve spies into the land that He had promised the children of Israel. They came back reporting that it was a magnificent country, but that the people living there were too powerful to overcome. Caleb and Joshua felt differently. They believed God had more power. They wanted to go in and possess what God had promised. They told the people that the Lord loved them and would keep them safe. The people then wanted to stone Caleb and Joshua for standing up for what they believed. God was so displeased with the people that they had to spend forty years in the wilderness. Those that were twenty years of age and older, except for Caleb and Joshua, never made it to the Promised Land. But, even Caleb and Joshua had to suffer the **Consequences** and stay in the wilderness for the forty years. People often suffer from others' mistakes. We are responsible not only for ourselves, but for others in the choices we make.

Consequences

We influence others
With choices we make.
No one lives to himself.
Our actions can cause others' hearts to ache.

There is always some
Consequence to pay
When we or a loved one
Are led astray.

It is important
To pray before making a decision,
Otherwise we can cause
Great split and division.

Shared blessings result
When making a right choice;
By doing so we
Make others rejoice.

So we need to remember
There is always some consequence.
Our deeds will show
In the evidence.

Caleb said, "We should go up and take possession of the land, for we can certainly do it. But the men who had gone with him said, "We can't attack those people; they are stronger than we are." Num. 13:30b-31 NIV

"That night all the people of the community raised their voices and wept." "Why is the Lord bringing us to this land only to let us fall by the sword?" Num. 14:1 & 3a NIV

The Lord said, "not one of them will ever see the land I promised on oath to their forefathers." But because my servant Caleb has a different spirit and follows me wholeheartedly, I will bring him into the land he went to, and his descendants will inherit it." Num. 14:23a & 24 NIV

"For forty years-one year for each of the forty days you explored the land-you will suffer for your sins and know what it is like to have me against you." Num. 14:34 NIV

Teachable Hearts

I enjoy watching my youngest granddaughter as she learns new things. There is such an eagerness to do what her sisters do. She has an open mind. She's observing. There will come a time when she will probably say, ``I'll do it'' and not want help. Even then I hope she realizes that sometimes we all need help.

Many people stop learning, as they get older. They think they already know it all. How sad! What a waste! To stop learning is to start dying. I believe God will continue to teach us something new if we will only ask and be open with **Teachable Hearts.**

Teachable Hearts

We can be taught
When we have a hunger to learn.
Willing spirits are needed
And hearts that yearn.

God can take available minds
And teachable hearts
And use them in His plan for
His message to impart.

We can be useable
If we show patience and trust.
God can take imperfection
And always adjust.

We can have on job training
If we are faithful and steady.
God wants to use us.
He is waiting and ready.

``And the Lord said unto Moses, Come up to me in the mount, and be there: and I will give thee tables of stone, and a law, and commandments which I have written; that thou mayest teach them. And Moses went into the midst of the cloud, and gat him up into the mount: and Moses was in the mount forty days and forty nights." Ex. 24:12&18 KJV

"And the Lord spake unto Moses face to face, as a man speaketh unto his friend. And he turned again unto camp: but his servant Joshua, the son of Nun, a young man, departed not out of the tabernacle." Ex. 33:11 KJV

(Joshua had a hunger to learn.)

Beyond Our Abilities

I feel very dependent on my husband. One of my greatest fears has been that someday he might have to go on to be with the Lord before I do. I know it is selfish to want to go first. I also know that isn't showing much trust in God.

God gave me a great experience three years ago. I wanted to go to Sweden to see our exchange student that had lived with my husband, youngest daughter, and myself in 1986-1987. She had given birth to her first child. I wanted to be with her. I wanted to see my new ``grandson''. I discussed it with my husband. He wasn't able to go because of work. I don't like to do these things without him, plus I am not the type. I'm scared! Now maybe it isn't a big thing for some, but it was a major thing for me. What if I had a panic attack right there in a foreign airport where I had to change airplanes? What if I couldn't find my way to my next plane? What if I missed my plane like my husband and I did ten years before when we went together to see Maria? Still, I felt a great desire to go. I made my reservation. My husband took me to the Atlanta airport. Before he left me there I had struck up a conversation with a young lady that was going to my destination. What a relief! I would just ask her for help or follow where she went. Maria met me when I arrived in Sweden. I had a wonderful week with all her family and friends. Then it was time to make the trip back home. What if I still couldn't handle changing planes in what I felt was the world's biggest airport? I wouldn't have that young lady that helped me before. I met a young businessman that sat with me on the small plane going from

Gothenburg, Sweden, to London. He said he would help, but he had to go to a different terminal. When I arrived in London I had to ride a shuttle bus. After getting off I spotted a lady holding up a homemade sign that said, ATLANTA. I went to her and said, ``Can you help me?'' She said, ``What is your name?'' I said, ``Glenda Chatham.'' She turned a clipboard over and it had one name on it. It read, GLENDA CHATHAM. She said, ``I am here to take you to your plane.'' I walked beside her past many airport shops and restaurants and down long hallways. She took me all the way to my gate. Fifteen minutes later I was on my plane coming back to the states. I sat there before take off with chills of excitement, thinking WOW! How God does work. God goes **Beyond Our Abilities.**

Beyond Our Abilities

God never asks us to do the impossible
Without first providing help.
There's never been a promise made
That He has not kept.

Giving God controlling interest
Will bring us peace.
No matter what we have to face
God's blessings will never cease.

We need to trust God's ability.
There is no better deal.
He has something to offer
That no one can rob or steal.

``Finally, my brethren, be strong in the Lord, and in the power of his might. Put on the whole Armour of God, that ye may be able to stand against the wiles of the devil.'' Eph. 6:10-11 KJV

Door of Escape

Isaiah 64:6 says, "We are all as an unclean thing, and all our righteousnesses are as filthy rags; and we all do fade as a leaf: and our iniquities, like the wind, have taken us away." Romans 3:10 says, "There is none righteous, no, not one." It is written in Romans 3:23, "For all have sinned, and come short of the glory of God." Then in Romans 6:23 it says, "For the wages of sin is death; but the gift of God is eternal life through Jesus Christ our Lord." Last of all in Romans 10:9-10 it says, That if thou shalt confess with thy mouth the Lord Jesus, and shalt believe in thine heart that God hath raised him from the dead, thou shalt be saved. For with the heart man believeth unto righteousness; and with the mouth confession is made unto salvation." WOW! He made a **Door of Escape** for everyone who is willing to take it.

Door Of Escape

There is a door of escape
For every temptation that we face.
It was opened on Calvary
When God shed His amazing grace.

God has placed it before us.
It is a door that only we can shut.
It makes no difference the sin
Or how deep is our rut.

Whatever happens in life,
No matter how great the temptation,
If we will only believe,
God will be there without hesitation.

It takes only our willingness to let Him come
through.
A provision has already been made.
When Jesus died upon the cross.
The price of our sins was paid.

"Behold, I stand at the door, and knock: if any man hear my voice, and open the door, I will come in to him, and will sup with him, and he with me." Rev.4: 20 KJV

Reflections

On a trip to Montana my husband and I went to Glacier Park. We stopped and took pictures at Lake McDonald. The **Reflections** of the glaciers in the lake were so clear that when I had my pictures developed I couldn't tell if I was holding the picture upside down or right side up. It was a beautiful sight. I hope my life reflects that I have Jesus in my heart.

Reflections

As I stood by a beautiful lake
And saw the glaciers' reflections,
I thought about life
And its different directions.

I was in a panoramic setting
When I saw this awesome mirror.
I reflected on my life,
To view it more clearer.

It was the end of the day.
I was viewing snow-capped peaks.
I thought about how God's
Creation was so unique.

I wondered what reflections
I had made on this earth.
Was I fulfilling God's plan
For me since my birth?

"And God called the dry land Earth; and the gathering together of the waters He called Seas: and God saw that it was good." Gen. 1:10 KJV

"It is good neither to eat flesh, nor drink wine, nor any thing whereby thy brother stumbleth, or is offended, or is made weak." Rom. 14:21 KJV

Unopened Letters

In the days before computers and e-mail it was nice to go to the mailbox and find a letter from someone I cared for. When I was away at college I could expect a letter from my mother every Tuesday. She would write and share with me what was going on back home. My fiancé wrote me even more often. I received about three letters a week from him. I take those letters out ever so often and re-read them. They still warm my heart. When I moved five hundred miles from home, I would sit by the Saint Johns River in Sanford, Florida, and read letters from my grandmother back in Georgia. She would let me know how much she missed me. I received a letter from my granddaughter, Hannah, a couple of days ago. She lives two thousand miles away. It felt good to hold the letter in my hand just knowing she had held it in hers. I get excited when my exchange student, Maria, from Sweden sends me something in the mail, especially when it contains pictures of her two little boys, Alex and Robin. I enjoy hearing from loved ones. I enjoy getting e-mails on-line, but there is just something special about those letters sent the old fashioned way.

God inspired letters and had them written to us centuries ago. In His word, the Bible, He shares His love, how he wants us to live, how he is preparing a place and is going to come again and take us home with Him. I can't imagine having **Unopened Letters** received from those I have loved over the years. I love to study God's word. It makes me feel close to Him.

Unopened Letters?

When my husband sent me love letters
Before becoming his bride,
I would never have dreamed of
Tossing them aside.

I even open letters marked occupant
From people who don't care.
I think, well maybe,
They have something to share.

I check for e-mails
When I go on-line.
If the postman delivers a check,
I certainly don't decline.

Many years ago there were letters
Sent from God up above.
No message could be greater and
So full of love.

How could I ever not
Open those letters?
The only thing possible
Is that they make my life better.

"Study to show thyself approved unto God, a workman that needeth not to be ashamed, rightly, dividing the word of truth." 2 Tim. 2:15 KJV

"Thy word have I hid in my heart that I might not sin against thee." Ps: 119:11 KJV

God Makes Tears

Man has the ability to accomplish many things. He has built empires and acquired worldly wealth. The God of the universe gave man this power. But only God can create feelings. Only God can create life. Only **God Makes Tears** of joy and feelings of love.

God Makes Tears

People are smart.
God has given them abilities.
With all the knowledge
Have come many possibilities.

Technology has been developed
Because of men's and women's intellect.
Many buildings have resulted
Because of great architects.

People often even
Explore out in space
And make it back to earth
Because of God's Grace.

Only God can make tears
Of joy and feelings of love.
People are limited.
Those things only come from above.

``They that sow in tears shall reap in joy.'' Ps. 126:5 KJV

``The joy of the Lord is your strength.'' Neh. 8:10c KJV

``God is love.'' 1John 4:8b KJV

Take A Stand

"A certain man went down from Jerusalem to Jericho, and fell among thieves, which stripped him of his raiment, and wounded him, and departed, leaving him half dead. And by chance there came down a certain priest that way: And when he saw him, he passed by on the other side. And likewise a Levite, when he was at the place, came and looked on him, and passed by on the other side. But a certain Samaritan, as he journeyed came where he was: and when he saw him, he had compassion on him, and went to him, and set him on his own beast, and brought him to an inn, and took care of him; And on the morrow when he departed, he took out two pence, and gave them to the host, and said unto him, Take care of him; and whatsoever thou spendest more, when I come again, I will repay thee. Which now of these three, thinkest thou, was neighbour unto him that fell among the thieves?" These were the words of Jesus in Luke 10:30-36.

Why did the priest and Levite pass by on the other side? Why do Christians close their eyes to things that are going on that are wrong without even questioning? When others are wounded why do Christians pass by on the other side?

There is a time to speak out and a time to be quiet, but at least pray for that guidance and then follow God's leadership. Care! **Take a stand!**

Take a Stand

When there's trouble,
Take time to pray.
Don't turn your back
And run away.

Don't let others
Experience grief
Because you weren't willing
To show your beliefs.

It is important
To not start a riot.
Know when to speak.
Know when to be quiet.

Know when to listen
And not cause hurt,
But, also, take a stand.
Don't be an introvert.

Be responsible.
Don't have others misunderstand.
First pray to God.
Then take a stand.

``God is our refuge and strength, a very present help in trouble.'' Ps. 46:1 KJV
``But Jonah rose up to flee'' Jonah 1:3a KJV

``Who will stand up for me against the workers of iniquity?" Ps. 94:16b KJV

``To every thing there is a season, and a time to every purpose under the heaven: a time to keep silence, and a time to speak:" Eccl. 3:1&3:7b KJV

``For by faith ye stand." 2 Cor.1: 24b KJV

Lost Eyes and Ears

It is true as Isaiah 64:6 says that our righteousnesses are as filthy rags, but it is also true that if we are children of God we have been sanctified in Christ Jesus. We are His saints. We are to be Christlike. We are to follow His example. There is no excuse for what we as church members are doing today. Satan is having a good time in our churches with God's children. He is not able to pluck us out of God's hands, (John 10:28-29) but we are allowing him to destroy our influence on a lost and dying world. What are **Lost Eyes and Ears** seeing and hearing when they observe those who claim to be Christians?

Lost Eyes And Ears

Lost eyes–
Lost ears–
What do they see?
What do they hear?

Do God's children
Gossip, slander, and hurt?
When others are talking
Are Christians alert?

Do those who are lost
See Christians as rude?
Do they even see
Them having feuds?

What do the lost see?
Do they see Christians peaceful and content
Or do they see them
Restless and with much dissent?

Do they hear words
That should never be repeated?
Are there conversations between
God's children that even become heated?

There's a lost world
That's going to hell.
Will the lost listen
When God's children tell?

``We put no stumbling block in anyone's path, so that our ministry will not be discredited. Rather, as servants of God we commend ourselves in every way: in great endurance; in troubles, hardships and distresses; in beatings, imprisonments and riots; in hard work, sleepless nights and hunger; in purity, understanding, patience and kindness; in the Holy Spirit and in sincere love;'' 2 Cor. 6:3-6 NIV

``Make up your mind not to put any stumbling block or obstacle in your brother's way.'' Rom. 14:13b NIV

God's Plumb Line

A builder would not attempt to build without making sure his walls were plumb. He needs his foundation to be sound and his walls straight. He has his plans. God, too, has his standards that must be met. He does not accept any, but His own. Only through the blood of His Son can we become His child. There is no other way. We can never be good enough on our own no matter how hard we work lest any one of us would want to boast. (Read Ephesians 2:9) Acts 4:12 tells us there is not ``salvation in any other: for there is none other name under heaven given among men, whereby we must be saved.'' God, our builder, has only one set of plans. He has His own **Plumb Line**.

God's Plumb Line

A plumb line is a cord
With a weight tied at one end.
It is used to measure accuracy
For what the builder intends.

God has His standards
For all His creation.
He doesn't waver
Or accept imitations.

God expects His people
To be "built true to plumb".
His way is perfect.
He knows the desired outcome.

God's Word-the Bible
Is an instrument of measure.
If it is used
It will bring God pleasure.

God's the perfect builder.
He will never fail.
Using Him as a point of reference
Makes the Christian's life prevail.

``The Lord said unto me, Amos, what seest thou? And I said, A plumbline. Then said the Lord, Behold, I will set a plumbline in the midst of my people Israel:''
Amos 7:8a KJV

110

In Different Shoes

It is hard for me to understand the ways of some people. Sometimes I don't even understand why I do the things I do. Families differ in values and beliefs that they teach their children. I have read that children from the same family are different simply because of their birth order. Wherever we are coming from it is important that our focus be on Christ. Through Him we are better able to accept one another. We all are walking **In Different Shoes.**

In Different Shoes

As we travel this life through,
We walk with feet in different shoes.
We go many miles along the way.
Lord, let us allow You to guide each day.

Often skies are gray or blue,
As we walk in different shoes.
May we seek our Savior's will
In worship time that's still.

Lord, help us not to hurt or bruise,
As we walk in different shoes;
But may we each and everyone
Remember daily what You have done.

"But why dost thou judge thou brother? Or why dost thou set at nought thy brother? For we shall all stand before the judgment seat of Christ. Let us not therefore judge one another anymore: but judge this rather, that no man put a stumbling block or an occasion to fall in his brother's way." Rom. 14:10,13 KJV

Life Is A Gift

Life: A gift from God. Each of us has been given a special gift when we were born. Some may feel more limited than others, but those like Joni Eareckson Tada with her limited physical abilities have proven what can be done with the gift of life. Joni was left as a quadriplegic after a diving accident in 1967. She has affected thousands of lives through her ministries. God has blessed her and she has given Him the credit.

God created each of us with a purpose in mind. **Life Is A Gift**. It is not meant to be wasted.

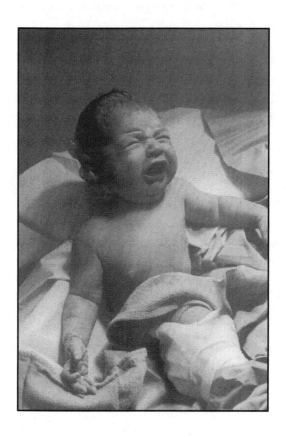

Life Is A Gift

Life is a gift
We don't need to waste.
Responsibilities on each of us
Have been placed.

As long as we're here
There is a job to do.
We need to remember our Maker
And to Him be true.

If we are God's children,
Our lives will never end.
We need to search daily
For how our lives we should spend.

Lord, Help us seek Your way-
Not go out on our own.
May You be pleased with us
And our timepieces You have loaned.

``Do not neglect your gift, which was given to you through a prophetic message when the body of elders laid their hands on you. Be diligent in these matters: give yourselves wholly to them, so that everyone may see your progress. Watch your life and doctrine closely. Persevere in them, because if you do, you will save both yourself and your hearers." 1 Tim. 4:14-16 NIV

Acquaintance or Friend?

A friend is someone whom you enjoy being around; someone you know well. A friend is someone who knows all about you and still cares for you. An acquaintance is someone you know, but have not developed a close relationship with. Many claim to know there is a God and even believe that some day they will automatically go to heaven when they die not realizing they have to have a personal relationship, knowing Jesus as friend and Savior. Even Satan knows Jesus, but not as a friend.

There is no better friend than Jesus. He gave His life that we may have an eternal relationship with Him. Even some say that wasn't enough, that He died too soon. While He was still on the cross He said, ``It is finished.'' I believe He really meant it was. Is He your **Acquaintance or Friend?**

Acquaintance Or Friend?

Do you really know God?
Have you accepted His Son?
Do you know that they're the same?
Do you know they are one?

Jesus died on the cross
So we could have salvation.
He wants us as friends.
He desires communication.

Satan knows there is a God.
His existence even he believes.
Satan doesn't want us to be God's friends,
So he is out to deceive.

On the cross Jesus said,
"It's finished" for evermore.
Don't let others tell you He died to soon
And that there is more.

Jesus wants us to know Him personally
And have Him come into our hearts.
He wants us to trust Him as Savior
And for us never to be apart.

``I and the Father are one.'' John 10:30 KJV

"If ye had known me, ye should have known my Father also: and from henceforth ye know him, and have seen him." John 14:7 KJV

"When Jesus therefore had received the vinegar, he said, It is finished: and he bowed his head, and gave up the ghost." John 19:30 KJV

"Thou believest the there is one God; thou doest well: the devils also believe, and tremble." James 2:19 KJV

"That if thou shalt confess with thy mouth the Lord Jesus, and shalt believe in thine heart that God hath raised from the dead, thou shalt be saved. For with the heart man believeth unto righteousness; and with the mouth confession is made unto salvation." Rom. 10:9-10 KJV

To Everything There Is A Season

It is hard to believe I am a grandmother. Sometimes it seems only yesterday that I was a child spending time with my own grandmothers. Now those dear ladies have gone to be with the Lord.

I remember being a youth and sharing dreams for the future. Now when I see those childhood friends they have aged and turned gray and yet in some ways are still the same.

My once beautiful mother is now an elderly lady with a beautiful smile.

Time has flown by so quickly. Many of my loved ones have passed away. My own grandchildren do not know many of those who were so dear to me and yet they and the ones gone are a big part of who I am.

I miss those who are no longer with me, but love watching my very youngest grandbaby dancing to some music and everyone laughing as she tries to say a new word. **To Everything There Is A Season.**

To Every Thing There Is A Season

No one has seen God's face,
But His handiwork is all about.
After touching a new born babe,
How could anyone have a doubt?

Whether it be the winter of life
Or whether it be the spring,
God gives new beginnings.
He has a time for everything.

As long as there is life,
There can be a testimony.
God can use the most feeble
To show He isn't phony.

A smile from an elderly mother
Who still shows her love,
Has to be a message
That God, too, smiles from above.

God's creations are awesome.
Take a look around.
There's beauty in a rainbow.
Flowers are covering the ground.

Yes, there is a time to be born
And also a time to die,
But God is all knowing.
Nothing is hidden from His eye.

"To every thing there is a season, and a time to every purpose under the heaven: a time to be born, and a time to die." Ecc. 3:1-2a KJV

"A time to weep, and a time to laugh; a time to mourn, and a time to dance." Ecc. 3:4 KJV

"He hath made every thing beautiful in his time: also he hath set the world in their heart, so that no man can find out the work that God maketh from the beginning to the end." Ecc. 3:11 KJV

Patience

Waiting is hard for me. I want unpleasant times to be over ``yesterday''. I have learned that life does not work that way. I won't say that I still don't become obsessed with some of my problems or that I am not impatient, but my prayer life has changed. I don't blame God for discomforts that come my way. I don't inwardly throw temper tantrums as I did in years passed. I still suffer hurts, but I now ask the Lord for help through bad times. I know He only wants the best for me. He doesn't cause my conflicts, but neither does He take away my freedom of will or that of my inflictor if another causes the pain. He will be there for me. He will show me my faults and work with me to correct them if I ask. He will help me endure my burdens. He will lighten my load. It is still very difficult, but I have hope of some day having more **Patience**.

Patience

To endure without complaint
Is often hard for me to do.
I want to be objective
And see other's points of view.

I want to show patience
In waiting for a delay.
I want to seek my Lord's desires
And remember the need to pray.

``Wherefore seeing we also are compassed about with so great a cloud of witnesses, let us lay aside every weight, and the sin which doth so easily beset us, and let us run with patience the race that is set before us.''
 Heb.12: 1 KJV

``But if we hope for that we see not, then do we with patience wait for it.'' Rom.8: 25 KJV

``That ye be not slothful, but followers of them who through faith and patience inherit the promises.''
Heb.6: 12 KJV

``For ye have need of patience, that, after ye have done the will of God, ye might receive the promise.''
Heb.10: 36 KJV

122

Rebirth

God blessed my husband, Fred and me with the births of three daughters: Faith, Joy, and Rebekah. They have given birth to nine daughters. Now we are experiencing the "rebirth" of each of these children as we did that of their mothers. It was wonderful news when Rachel, the oldest granddaughter, announced her decision to accept Christ as her personal Savior. After our granddaughter Lydia accepted Jesus as Lord of her life, she led her younger sister, Mary, to the Lord. We have received this news many times over the passed few years and look forward to the day that circle is complete. Birth is precious. **Rebirth:** GLORIOUS!

Rebirth

Each time there is a birth
It should be a blessed event.
Every child that is born
Should be considered heaven sent.

To be nurtured in a Christian home,
Knowing God as their creator,
Is a right every child deserves.
There is nothing greater.

The word of God says
If a child is raised in the way it should go
That it will not depart from that way
When it is old.

I know of no sweeter sound
Than the cry heard at a child's birth
Unless it is the announcement when it is older
That God's creation has received a "rebirth".

``Train a child in the way he should go; and when he is old, he will not depart from it.'' Pro. 22:6 KJV

``But as many as received him. To them gave he power to become the sons of God, even to them that believe on his name:'' John 1:12 KJV

``For whosoever shall call upon the name of the Lord shall be saved.'' Romans 10:13 KJV

124

Reunion Day

I used to get so excited when my cousins from out of state came to visit. Most of my cousins lived within walking distance. I was just as excited to see them. Those were the cousins I went on vacations with. All the aunts and uncles would pack us into cars and we would go to the beach for a few days each summer. When I went away to a small Christian College I got so close to everyone they seemed like another group of cousins.

My husband and I moved around a few years after we married and made some great friends in each new place. Now many years later those friends are scattered miles away. Some of my own children and grandchildren are two thousand miles away. Even though some of the cousins that used to live near by are now also hundreds of miles apart a majority of us met at the beach a few months back.

My college friends got together for a fortieth reunion and stayed in the dormitory together. Many of us had married each other. It was like being back home with family. Since the college reunion a couple of years ago we are keeping in close touch and have a prayer chain going for one another's needs.

For our fortieth wedding anniversary my husband and I visited many of the places we used to live. We visited dear friends and again the years gone by just seemed to disappear.

Many aunts, uncles, and even a couple of cousins have now gone on to be with the Lord. Many other dear friends that have been a big part of my life have died. It hurts not to be closer to my daughter and grandchildren that are so far away. An exchange student that is now back in her own country is greatly missed. But, there is coming a reunion

125

day. I will see many of my loved ones together. Many I will introduce to each other. My greatest friend and brother I will come face to face with for the first time. JESUS. What a great **Reunion Day** that will be!

Reunion Day

Lord, I like family reunions
And being together with those I love.
As I grow older I think more often
Of the reunion that will some day be above.

I wonder how it will be
To feast and fellowship every day,
With no sad departures;
Where no one goes away.

When children grow up here
And scatter about this earth,
It is very difficult to accept, Lord
When they have been with us since their birth.

Lord, It's awesome to think
I will be with You face to face,
And have that physical contact
Of my Maker's glorious embrace.

As a child, Lord, I remember
My elders often letting out a shout.
Now as I am getting older
I am beginning to understand what it was all about.

Lord, I thank You
For the promise of a great reunion day.
And while I have to wait, Lord,
I thank You for the privilege to pray.

``In my Father's house are many mansions: if it were not so I would have told you. I go to prepare a place for you. And if I go to prepare a place for you, I will come again, and receive you unto myself;" John 14:2-3 KJV

A New Garden

What is Heaven going to be like? I know God creates the very best. The Garden of Eden must have been a beautiful place. God said it was very good. It had everything mankind needed. God even took walks through the garden Himself.

My mother's cousin Albert was talking about heaven the other day. He said, ``Just think, when we get to heaven we are going to see Abraham and Moses.'' Then he paused and said, ``But Jesus is going to outshine them all.''

I remember as a child hearing a dear elderly lady shout anytime she heard the preacher talking about Heaven. It made chills run up my spine. I didn't feel she was showing off. I felt she was just getting little glimpses of heaven because she would be going home soon.

I believe Jesus has gone to prepare a place for us just like He said He would. He is planting **A New Garden.**

A New Garden

In the beginning
God created a garden.
There He placed
The first man and woman.

The garden had trees
That were pleasing when viewed.
They were a resource:
A great menu for food.

Everything therein
Did God beautify.
There was nothing
He failed to supply.

God's presence was there
In the cool of the day.
God loved His creation.
Then mankind chose to disobey.

Sin entered in
And hearts became harden.
God was saddened
And banished them from the garden.

God hated sin,
But loved woman and man.
Because of His grace
Came a redemption plan.

Jesus died on a cross
To redeem all who obey.
By choosing His plan,
God's creation has the
Promise of again being
In His presence in
The cool of the day.

``Nevertheless we, according to his promise, look for new heavens and a new earth, wherein dwelleth righteousness.'' Peter 3:13 KJV

``For all have sinned, and come short of the glory of God; Being justified freely by his grace through the redemption that is in Christ Jesus: Whom God hath set forth to be a propitiation through faith in his blood, to declare his righteousness for the remission of sins that are past, through the forbearance of God; To declare, I say at this time his righteousness: that he might be just, and the justifier of him which believeth in Jesus. Where is boasting then? It is excluded. By what law? Of works? Nay: but by the law of faith.'' Rom.3: 23-27 KJV

Neither by the blood of goats and calves, but by his own blood he entered in once into the holy place, having obtained redemption for us." Heb. 9:12 KJV

"In my Father's house are many mansions: if it were not so, I would have told you. I go to prepare a place for you. And if I go and prepare a place for you, I will come again, and receive you unto myself; that where I am, there ye may be also." John 14:2-3 KJV

"And the building of the wall of it was of jasper: and the city was pure gold, like unto clear glass. And the foundations of the wall of the city were garnished with all manner of precious stones. And the twelve gates were twelve pearls; every several gate was of one pearl: and the street of the city was pure gold, as it were transparent glass." Rev. 21:18-19a, 21-22 KJV